S0-CRS-763

So to
Speak

a feminist journal of language and art

Spring 2014

So to Speak

Spring 2014 (vol. 23, no. 1)

Printed on recycled paper

ISBN: 978-0-9801309-7-3

Subscriptions and all other correspondence may be addressed to *So to Speak*, George Mason University, 4400 University Drive, MSN 2C5, Fairfax, VA 22030-4444.

Subscriptions: $7/sample issue, $12/one year, $22/two years

We can be found online at http://sotospeakjournal.org and contacted via email at sts@gmu.edu.

Submissions: We welcome all work relating to feminism. Please submit no more than five (5) poems at a time; all forms are invited. Limit fiction and nonfiction to 4,500 words. We welcome collaborations. All submissions should be sent electronically through our submission manager. For more detailed guidelines and for contest information, visit our website at http://sotospeakjournal.org. Our reading period is from August 15 through October 15 for the Spring issue and from January 15 through March 15 for the Fall issue.

Cover art: "Part of My Body is Missing" by Alexandra Zahedi Delafkaran

The editors would like to thank Jennifer Atkinson, all the authors and artists who submitted to our journal, David Carroll, Kathryn Mangus, the Phoebe staff, William Miller, the Fall for the Book Festival staff, the editorial circle that founded So to Speak (Jamy Bond, Sara Brown, Leslie Bumstead, Jean Donnelly, Colleen Kearney Rich, Isadora Lector, Stephanie Muller, and Rebecca Wee), and all past editors of the journal.

So to Speak: a feminist journal of language and art is committed to representing the work of writers and artists from diverse perspectives and experiences and does not discriminate on the basis of race, class, gender, age, religion, sexual orientation, culture of origin, disability, political affiliation, marital or parental status, Vietnam-era veteran status, or similar characteristics.

So to Speak is published bi-annually in print at George Mason University and annually online at http://sotospeakjournal.org. Opinions expressed by authors and editors do not necessarily reflect the official views of the university.

All rights reserved. No material herein may be reprinted by any means, recorded or quoted, other than for review purposes, without the express permission of the authors or artists, to whom all rights revert after serial publication.

So to
SPEAK

a feminist journal of language and art

EDITOR	Michele K. Johnson
MANAGING EDITOR	Erin McDaniel
ASSISTANT EDITOR	Christina Elaine Collins
FICTION EDITOR	Elizabeth Egan
NONFICTION EDITOR	Jessie Szalay
POETRY EDITOR	Amber L. Cook
ART EDITOR	Ceci Cole McInturff
BLOG EDITOR	Sheryl Rivett
ASSISTANT FICTION EDITOR	Julie Dickson
ASSISTANT NONFICTION EDITOR	Alexandra Ghaly
ASSISTANT POETRY EDITOR	Alicia K. Padovich
ASSISTANT BLOG EDITOR	Paula Beltrán

FICTION READERS	Marissa D'Orazio
	Karolina Gajdeczka
	Paul Michiels
	Lina Patton
	David Robinson
	Shannon Rosenblat
NONFICTION READERS	Eric Botts
	Karolina Gajdeczka
	Rajpreet Heir
POETRY READERS	Sonnee Barna
	Anya Creightney
	A. Moriah Jones
	James Merrifield
	Ryan Meyer
	Sarah Winn

CONTENTS

CONTENTS

VISUAL ART

CONTRIBUTORS

CONTEST JUDGES

SPRING 2014 POETRY CONTEST
REMARKS BY BETH ANN FENNELLY

WINNER: "Late Light," by Carol Quinn

"Late Light" is a rangy, ambitious elegy that traces the trajectory of grief. The speaker seems to be a woman mourning the death of her stepbrother, and the parts of the poem move through a variety of tones and emotions. We begin with memories of the rebellious young man who protested against Ronald Reagan in a Mormon church, was abused by his father, and ran away from home. The poet then depicts the stepbrother's death in a hospital, capturing the deep mystery of the end of life: "The change seems less than the breath / at a dandelion." After his death, the poet switches her address from second person, "Ubiquitous you," to third person: "He lasted until summer solstice. / He never went to Europe." We end with the funeral, sharing the speaker's rage and bitterness at the Bishop's glib sermon and at the burial where "[in] the hills of Calabasas / the dead are as close / as sprinkler systems and landfill." This is a moving, thoughtful, elegant poem.

HONORABLE MENTION: "A Black Bird with Snow-Covered Red Hills," by Jessica Jacobs

"A Black Bird with Snow-Covered Red Hills" is rather like the painter the poem portrays: It shows remarkable technical skill and also a charming, compelling vision. Told from the persona of Georgia O'Keeffe writing to her distant lover, we see the painter moving through her solitary landscape with power and resolve, dedicated to the art that demands her complete focus. Two-thirds of the way through, the poem makes a delightful move. O'Keeffe sleeps "knees tucked so tight to my chest / I hold my own soles, Cannon-ball!" This provides the springboard for the surprise of the final image. Through the magic of the imagination, her cannonball splashes her far-away lover "taking sun on the dock." The poem ends, "Love, / come join me in this water." I am only too glad to accept this invitation.

Late Light

for my stepbrother
(May 3, 1963–June 20, 2012)

1

You wanted oils, song, and turpentine.
You wanted priming—for distillations of fire—
but fixed engines (with a sculptor's hands).

The world is singed between the lines.
Airwaves become a wavering of the air.

A window closes in a hospital room.
The frequencies of song pass through
the flickering exhaust—

but they are only recordings now.
The change seems less than the breath
at a dandelion,
                        less than the sexual release
of a man who thinks he can't become a father
because he's too young to become a father,

who will beat the son who's born anyway.
And you (the son) would joke anyway.

But when you ran away—Motor City 5
and Zeppelin carrying over the walls—
when you held your bottle up to the sky,
the colors were the same: wheatfield,
stil de grain, grenache, chardonnay.
Tonight the colors pour like libations
beyond the Ventura Freeway—

the TV antennas and cell phone towers
like the seeds of a dandelion
that were broadcast over dry, Mojave stones.

2

Step-: from *steop, steupa, steif*—
old words for *loss, bereft, pushed out.*
I knew your escape routes but waited.
There were rumors of wars and other reasons
for leaving home. In a Mormon church
you testified (*I know who 666 is:*
Ronald Wilson Reagan). I expected the end
of freeways and Smith's Food King,
but hoped the wild oats and fig trees would
outlast our house.

This was before
cineplexes and gated, duplicate fiefdoms
(world without end, amen). There were only
the chaparral of empty lots and foothills,
and orange groves no one tended any longer
(sweetness of forgotten, blossoming branches).

You wanted to go to college. Your father
my stepfather said *I'm not gonna pay*
for your ass to sit in a coffee shop.

The old man, who once beat his son's head
against a dresser for coming home drunk,
walks into the room and has to walk out again
when he sees you lying on a hospital bed.

I say this as if I had to remind you.
I say *you* as if I had to remind you.

Ubiquitous you so often away
I must now unlearn like childhood slang,
you slip in memory to *Dave, he.*

3

He lasted until the summer solstice.
He never went to Europe.
He didn't know the Sami, who
sometimes married our Finnish cousins,
believe the soul goes to the sun.

When I heard, I went up into the hills
where nothing had yet been built
and listened to the tall grass.
His mother died young:
oat cell carcinoma, named
for how it looks under a microscope—
like tassels of wild oats in the wind.
Now it goes by other names:
secretory granules,
neuroendocrine cancer.
He didn't know
they may have had the same disease.

Our cousins will light bonfires
on mountaintops tonight,
let the kids stay out all night.

4

Dear Bishop: Do not say *Death is not*
the worst thing with the body
before you, the widow you didn't know
before you in your church.
                              Look at the hills.
The seeds are already in us. They are

what we become: the blowing field, the stalks
rising and falling until they are just chaff.
We also become the sun they rise toward.

Bless wit that turns away the wrath
of the Yahwist and John of Patmos,
Alpha and Omega, Genesis and Revelation.
For I give you another law.

Bless six-foot-two stepbrothers
who used their strength
to lift small children off the ground.
For perfect love casteth out fear.

A backhoe has dug out just enough space
for a single coffin. It's like the way we slept
in the house that held eleven people.

Or nothing like it. The backhoe showers
its red dirt over him, but
he still doesn't seem far away.

In the hills of Calabasas
the dead are as close
as sprinkler systems and landfill.

Except ye turn, and become as little children—

We would lie down on the earth.
We would roll down these hills as we did
when we came to visit his mother's grave.

Love is not a desire for immortality
so much as a desire for the immortality
of others—
            that they might never suffer and die
and have to leave us.

But even the light loses its way
and scatters,
                    turning red
like the soil of Calabasas, red
like light through the lids of our eyes.

A Black Bird with Snow-Covered Red Hills

Georgia O'Keeffe [Abiquiu, NM; 1949]

After years shared at a distance,
I am already accustomed

to an empty bed.
I summon the dogs from the morning

melt, their garland of red prints
mudding the floors. Walls

breathe back the stove's heat.
As long as I am here, you can still be

in New York, grousing
about your bowels and feet.

I pull on overshoes, walk, sketch.
You lunch with old friends

at the gallery. I make dinner.
Read. Wear your sweater to bed,

the blue one. Fall asleep writing to you
in my head, of that day, the next,

knees tucked so tight to my chest
I hold my own soles, Cannon-ball!

through the night. And you
are there, taking sun on the dock,

sputtering as my lake-splash

startles you awake. Love,

come join me in this water.

Spring 2014 Nonfiction Contest
Remarks by Jana Richman

WINNER: "Notes on Sexual Nostalgia," by Marilyn Adler Papayanis

What is an essay and how does one measure the success of an essay? Those simple questions have provided fodder for debate since Frenchman Michel de Montaigne, the patron saint of essayists, began exploring his own existence on the page in the latter half of the sixteenth century.

Essayist Scott Russell Sanders writes that the essay form "allows for an examination of our most powerful and bewildering experiences." I clutch the word "examination" in Sanders' observation. An essay is not a personal journal entry, nor a simple accounting of one's experience. An essayist begins with the personal and tears into it with a curious mind—questioning, probing, and exploring—taking the reader on a journey of spontaneous discovery, and in doing so, touching the human experience in all of us.

"Notes on Sexual Nostalgia" achieves this through thoughtful and beautiful prose. Examining one woman's sexual identity from childhood through adolescence, from "purposeful promiscuity" through marriage, from widowhood to middle age, Marilyn Adler Papayanis reflects upon the sexual freedom of the sixties, questions the value of today's "hook-ups," explores the "intertextual" relationship between literature and desire, sex and creativity, and ponders the loss of sexual identity in the "absence of the desire to desire."

Notes on Sexual Nostalgia

When my husband died in November of 2004, I was barely 50. I don't believe we ever admitted to each other that he was dying, even as he lay, semiconscious, in a hospice bed. For two years we believed we could beat the diagnosis of pancreatic cancer and, at times, it seemed we might. My grief was like a hollow drum from which noiseless vibrations radiated outward, a vacant stillness within. Beyond the walls of my home, the world echoed like an empty room after the movers have come, not broom-clean, and still bearing the shadows cast by a fully inhabited life. I mourned not only the loss of my beloved companion, my intellectual partner, and the image of his robust pre-cancer self, but, over time, the grace of an embodied intimacy that was both so much more and so much less than sex.

Most of my life, I had been boy crazy; even as a four-year-old, I would play dead when one or another of my (much) older brother's attractive friends would come over. What constitutes "attractive" to a four-year old? Once, having wandered away from my family in Robert Hall, a popular men's clothing store of the time, I was found by a salesman unzipping the fly of a male dummy. My first serious crush was Sir Lancelot, a TV character of the 1950s. Then I was violently taken with Russ Tamblyn's naked body, wrapped in a leaf, when I saw the movie *Tom Thumb*. Like an old sticker, this image sits on its own page from the Golden Book of childhood.

At a bungalow colony in the Catskills, I learned from a group of older girls that boys don't buy the cow when they can get the milk for free. I was, I think, 12 years old. My mother told me to be careful with older boys who might not be able to "control" themselves. At night we would gather in someone's bungalow and slow dance to "Soldier Boy" and "Sealed with a Kiss" with the lights off. Did I feel an erection? Did I even know what an erection was? This was around 1965, the last year, maybe, we were going to "save it" for our husbands.

By the following summer, my friend and I were obsessed with sex, poetry, and the fathers who drove up on the weekends to rejoin their wives and children. There was a wild girl, an "artist," who spoke with nonchalance about "doing it." She was a counselor at the day camp. Was it only the year before that morality marched in lock step with the faux pearls and sweater sets in the fall issue of *Glamour*? I wrote a poem about one of those fathers. Finding him sitting alone one day at the lake, I showed it to him without, of course, identifying the poem's subject. I can't imagine what he was thinking or what synergistic powers propelled me towards him that summer afternoon. I do remember, with absolute clarity, the decision to approach him. It unfolds in slow motion. Sometimes I cringe when I think back on that preternaturally seductive self. Lolita's sister? Another sticker, but not in the Golden Book.

Coming of age in the '60s was a boon. Sex was everywhere and everywhere available. What I couldn't yet do I fantasized about; my fantasies became poems. I was an overripe figment of my own imagination, riding wave upon wave of hormonal turbulence into the Day-Glo scriptorium of wannabe confession. I channeled all the fury of sexual awakening into the fraught stillness of words. A stranger's glance on the subway, once taken in, could reverberate for days, could tremble at the tip of consciousness, like a glancing flame on sun-stoked skin. Let's call it, why not, a clitoral moment. A touch to the senses that rockets through consciousness to the place where imagination, embodied, bodies forth. I was prolific. I was provocative. Who couldn't spot Lolita's sister?

I lost my virginity thoughtlessly and early. My stomping ground was the long defunct Cafe Feenjon in Greenwich Village, a coffee house where musicians from the Levant played a thrilling fusion of Jewish, Greek, Arabic, and Turkish music till night tripped over the edge of dawn. Here, bellydancing was a couples dance. It was the sexiest place I could imagine. I indiscriminately pursued foreign men, regretting that there wasn't time enough to sleep with every dark handsome Greek that jumped ship in New York City. One would get deported only to be replaced by another and another. They were barely more than teenagers themselves. Between more or less steady, if short-term, partners, I let the laws of physical attraction have their way with me. I wasn't yet 17. Poetry languished.

Needless to say, I grew out of such intense and purposeful

promiscuity. I say purposeful because my "program" of sexual tuition was, to my way of thinking, an existential imperative. Chillingly precocious, I read Kazantzakis' *Zorba the Greek* through a heady cocktail of Sartre and Camus, binging as indiscriminately in the books as in the flesh. All my readings and misreadings were but fodder for an overactive imagination by now stoked with anticipation and impatience. I took my Bovaryism, warped by the distorting fevers of youth, as an intellectual challenge that was, at the same time, an assault on reason. I liked the daring quality of sexual adventurism. In the mid-to-late '60s, this was still outré, at least in the suburbs of Westchester. It grew to be a compelling aspect of self-definition.

Once the frenzy of sexual experimentation passed, a more normative period of "dating," or what passed for dating in the late '60s, ensued. I, like many others, came to take recreational sex more or less for granted. It never occurred to me that love was a prelude to sex, or its absence a bar to joyful indulgence. Indeed, having sex was like throwing spaghetti against a wall; sometimes it stuck. I never imagined that one could get bored, or even disgusted, with one's lover. It never entered my mind.

In time, I learned that when a lover became a boyfriend for any significant period of time, my lust turned mysteriously to aversion. I could awaken one day and find his touch toxic. If nothing ever came to surpass the breathless immediacy of a first embrace, so too did the well-practiced touch of a steady lover grow unbearable. These unmotivated aversions could not be overcome. Neither could they be understood. Still, it didn't much matter to me at the time. "Forever" would be reserved for the mythic One, and I was far from ready to settle down.

I slept with a lot of married men. Nothing excites lust quite like the flagrantly unavailable object of affection. Energetic seduction was my modus operandi. I remember prancing around my apartment, stark naked, to the amazement of a startled young attorney. I had never spoken to him until one day at the photocopy machine when I told him I had dreamt about him the night before. It was the truth. When I was sick with the flu, he called me every ten minutes, and I didn't get much rest. He was too clingy. Many years later, I would enjoy afternoon trysts with a lover in my tenement apartment on

28th Street. We would leave the office separately and he would await me up the block in a taxi. Sometimes he could really stay. We cooked. We took a bath. I thought he was the ONE, but I am eternally grateful that he never left his wife. With married men, sex is rarely boring.

Monica Lewinsky. Let me be perfectly clear about this. I would have done exactly the same thing. Of course, I would have lobbied strenuously for consummation, but, hey, he was The President.

And then, finally, I met the ONE. My so well-loved husband, long awaited and dying too soon, remained to me an object of such all-encompassing respect and adoration that the waning of desire, though painful I'm sure to him and certainly to me, became part of a shared journey of intimacy realized in manifold colors and forms. The barren space within this richly textured mosaic of emotional and intellectual bounty took on the shadings of poignancy and stubborn resiliency. The life-affirming nature of conjugal relations assumed a strident if unremittingly abstract quality. Affection and lust were experiential domains destined never again to coincide.

Then he died. After the leaden profundity of my loss began to lighten, mourning seemed to gravitate toward that barren space where riotous desire once ruled. Obsessively watching a special on PBS called *The Sixties* (an early My Music feature never repeated), I became fixated on Steppenwolf's very well-preserved lead singer, John Kay. From the depths of my shadowy half-life, I could see his outline in the brightness above. He extended his arm. My angel of grace. On an airplane I wrote a short story about a woman who finds herself on an airplane sitting next to a former rock star with whom she had had sex after a concert when she was a teenager. He does not remember the defining moment of her young existence. I experienced a different kind of high as the narrative came to life on the scraps of paper I pulled out of my bag to contain it. In that second-stage crucible of mourning, stories emerged and circled back in time to a sexual euphoria so pristine, so acute, that like a knife it cut through the damaged fibers of my life's dark tapestry. I captured them in healing words that lit the way forward in low-beam pearls of light.

As this unlikely muse graciously drew me up from the

shadows, I found myself wondering whether I would spend the rest of my life alone, whether my no-longer-young body would ever again approach the mindless delights of all-night sex. Passions—yes, I do remember—that abated only with the breach of a wakeful sun. It seemed an impossible idea. I ventured back to ballroom dancing, the only singles activity I was ever able to embrace without self-consciousness. I have been dancing all my life. The first time a man showed interest, I went home and wept. It was like another death. But other thoughts assailed me as well. "What lay under the well-tailored clothes of gray-haired / men, even / those not ravaged by cancer?" A poem was born. I called it "Widow's Weeds."

I was, it seemed, coming back. Slowly, I resumed my boy-crazy way of being, relaxing into that familiar state of obsession and anticipation. But being 50 is not the same as being 15. It seemed that my very identity as a sexual being was in question. No one lines up to court Lolita's granny. I did get my wish. A brief but heart-breaking affair—of an intensity matched only by the pathos of my last marital embrace—carried me forward, and backward, to the fantastical plenitude of much earlier days. I wondered what my ever-jealous husband would think, he who was honest enough to tell me (before he ever got sick) that he hoped I would never look for someone else to take his place should he be the first to go. Considering the 13-year age difference between us, it was likely that he would do so. "The dead," a friend told me, "are very forgiving." This avatar of sexual prowess didn't last long enough to get old.

I had an on-again, off-again relationship with a classical musician who, I am sure, suffered from Asperger's Syndrome. I met him on JDate. Though he was delightful in many ways, I bailed when I discovered that he had never given up cruising the dating sites. He was not wired for emotional intimacy. Even holding hands was a bridge too far. It was not worth the trouble, despite the unexpected (if risky) joys of sex with a man maybe three times my weight. Life is strange.

I met a man whose caged cockatiels hissed at me. The same man didn't bother to put his trousers on for our second date. Not that we had sex, you understand. I guess I was asking for it, driving 60 miles to see THE ONE (news flash: LIGHTNING DOESN'T

STRIKE TWICE) whose profile never hinted at deficits I was nevertheless fully prepared to overlook, having settled my affections on the fictional counterpart.

No stories cooled or consoled me during these misadventures, though the bird-man did inspire a poem or two. Afterward, in the long space of nonengagement, sex found its way into my scholarly work on popular music and film. Representations of sex are endlessly interesting to analyze, be they in prose, lyrics, or film. I have ever been haunted by the promise of arousal, the plunge into darkness, the coming back, the languor of skin-time. The '60s gave me all this. Now I'm 60.

In the sexual languishing of a post-post flower child, for whom virginity was just some trumped-up bling adorning the double standard, I wonder, sometimes, if it was the newness of the Sexual Revolution and not sex per se that made the idea of "doing it" so life-defining. The breaking of taboos was almost as intoxicating as the acts themselves. The aura of sex seemed to be infused with a narcotic of youthful abandon and risk. But it never felt risky. My mother tells me now she was so frightened for me because I never knew fear. For women, it was, to quote Shakespeare, "a brave new world." The Pill gave us safety from unwanted pregnancy, the clitoral orgasm threw open the doors of bliss. It seemed impossible, then, that sexual boredom, the stealth bomber of desire, lay in wait to ambush us in our newly found status as sexual beings.

I am old enough to remember the days when the idea of sex as something to be endured but not enjoyed was commonplace among married women of a certain age. Some of this was, no doubt, a cultural coding left over from earlier times when respectable women were deemed to have no sexual desires or needs, these being the province of "easy" women. But bodies, being first and foremost carnal entities, are bodies. I wonder now whether the first blush of sexual desire was as heady then as now, but that, over time, desire morphed into duty. Or perhaps, just as likely, lovers were ignorant as to the mechanics of female orgasm. Imagine trying to market a lust pill to women for whom sexual arousal was a dead end. And, even assuming that sex was fully satisfying, who was talking about sexual boredom back then? Who would dare?

Now there's a diagnosis: hypoactive sexual-desire disorder, or H.S.D.D. Women who suffer from this condition no longer desire their long-term partners. I found this out when I read "There May Be a Pill for That: The Pharmaceutical Quest to Give Women a Better Sex Life" in *The New York Times Magazine* (26 May, 2013). The author, Daniel Bergner, a staff writer for the magazine, reviews the science of female desire and the research being undertaken to produce a pill that will restore the "lust" balance between the sexes. Apparently women are far more susceptible to sexual boredom than men. It's not like falling out of love, which would be more straightforward. It's falling out of lust. The mythic One has become radioactive, even as he retains the status of beloved in every other way. The cause: monogamy.

That's what got me to thinking about the trajectory of my own sexual journey, from the unchartered abandon of the '60s, to the unanticipated fall from bliss when sexual desire is cut off at the knees, to the (once) unimaginable absence of the desire to desire. This is an abstract problem for me now. Nevertheless, the anxious juxtaposition of plenitude and impoverishment (like tectonic plates shifting uneasily against each other) has set off intermittent swells of sexual nostalgia. There is a poignant irony in this, or, if you like, an ironic poignancy. Sexual nostalgia. I'm not sure what that means anymore.

The problem, it turns out, is far more compelling than the solution. At 60, I straddle the divide between a healthy desire for sex and a "permissible" disinterest in pursing sexual relationships. From the far side of romance, I consider my options. Sure, it's conceivable that a wonderful man will come into my life; he will be smart and (to me) sexy, and, of course, he will be a great lover. I will, once again, know myself as a sexual being. There will be a certain continuity between the stages of my life. But how will I feel when desire starts to wane? When I start to practice "avoidance behaviors"? When I wish to lie in my bed alone and not worry about the desiring body shifting restlessly in the bed beside me.

Helping a much younger colleague, recently separated, set up a profile on Match.com, I remembered my own nervousness and anticipation the first time I submitted a profile and wondered how many frogs would dive for my golden bowl. Or, better yet, whether the prince himself would take the bait. After a flurry of interest (the trollers, it turns out, love novelty) I discovered that dating sites for the 50-plus woman are a toxic waste dump. Just imagine what radioactive scum survives and crawls out—the 30-year-olds who claim to find older women sexy (really?), the "never married" (why?), and the multitudes in pursuit of life "and all it has to offer" (demoralizing cliché). But being over 60, I am discovering, is a nonstarter, even in the swamplands of digital dating.

Nevertheless, my mind is now bedeviled with a persistent fantasy. I imagine myself absorbed in rapt conversation with an interesting and appropriate prospect. (I have never had such a first "date" since the one I had with my husband.) We sit at an outdoor café or a pub; the initial anxiety is over and we are both reassured that the imponderables of "chemistry" will not throw a damper on what looks to be a promising match. When he expresses the desire to see me again, I tell him, "Well, you know. It's like this. We will have passionate transcendent sex for, maybe, a year, after which time I will cringe when you approach me." I am my own wet blanket.

Now that H.S.D.D. has been identified and broadcast, I feel blighted. Any hope for future romance turns acrid. The power of naming! As it turns out, though, I am on the cusp of irrelevancy to the pathology itself. They don't even bother to tell us about the prevalence of H.S.D.D. among the 60-plus crowd. So I don't think this new pill is intended for those of us whose libidos may be considered worn out, but rather for our younger, premenopausal sisters. If E.D. is, to a great extent, a function of age, H.S.D.D. is clearly not. And, in truth, I'm not sure I desire desire anymore. It strikes me that there is a "natural" waning of the desire for sex—with anyone, just as there are other types of falling away that come with age, a winding down that is, for now at least, unavoidable. The desire to not even feel desire is something new to me. How ironic—*and* poignant—that the "cure" should be coming down the pike now.

I am grateful for having lived a lusty life. And lucky. By the time AIDS stole in to pollute the well, the free love generation had, for the most part, settled into some form of domesticity. Sex has been, and remains, the matrix of all my creative endeavors, from poetry and short stories to articles on zoning and pornography, female sexuality and Joni Mitchell's feminine aesthetic, to female orgasms and female sex tourism in the movies. For now, though, I am inclined to pass on the act itself. Even in fantasy, I do not get a buzz. I note, sadly, that today's so-called "hook-ups," at least the ones that occur on college campuses, are mediated by lots of booze. Hooking up is a way to have sex without relationships, and in this brave new world women are the ones rejecting emotional connection. For many female students on the fast track to professional success, boyfriends are an unnecessary distraction. But hookups don't sound too sexy to me. Women don't feel comfortable sleeping with men they don't know that well, so they get sloshed first. Consider a typical college frat party at the University of Pennsylvania:

"You go in, and they take you down to a dark basement," Haley, a blond, pink-cheeked senior recalled of her first frat parties in freshman year. "There's girls dancing in the middle, and then there's guys lurking on the sides and then coming and basically pressing their genitals up against you and trying to dance."

Dancing like that felt good but dirty, and like a number of girls, Haley said she had to be drunk in order to enjoy it.

"Dark basements?" "Lurkers?" "Dirty?" It sounds like a chamber of horrors! Where's the mating dance? Where's the flirtation? The anticipation? The *jouissance?* I, for one, would always want to be fully present for any sexual encounter. Why bother, otherwise? There was a whole article about this on the front page of the *New York Times* style section! (14 July, 2010)!

"Lust," the very sad (and ironically titled) short story by Susan Minot written in 1984 is another downer. This is mostly a list of boys with whom the dispirited teenage narrator has had sex, punctuated with joyless observations such as the following:

> The more girls a boy has, the better. He has a bright look, having reaped fruits, blooming. He stalks around, sure-shouldered, and you have the feeling he's got more in him, a fatter heart, more stories to tell. For a girl, with each boy it's as though a petal gets plucked each time.
>
> Then you get tired. You begin to feel diluted, like watered-down stew.

I often assign this story to my students, challenging them to question the logic (if not the socially-sanctioned "truth") of the girl's self-incriminatory perceptions. It's a good text for discussion, but sinks with the weight of didactic purity. I don't believe I ever felt like watered-down stew.

Which brings me to the intertextual nature of literature and desire. In the well of waking dreams where art and puberty met and intermingled, I sought—and found—multiple selves in texts from Austen to Whitman to Lawrence to Kazantzakis, texts that gave shape—not only in narrative possibility, but in texture, color, light, and shadow—to the incipient unfolding of sexuality. The context in which I came of age was one richly indebted to language, exquisitely sculpted and polished to a sensuous afterglow, fueled by imagination and ennobled by the simplicity of questions and the duplicity of answers beyond the merely provisional. It's how, in a way, sex and writing became so intertwined in my life, why I could so easily slide into articulation as a means of knowing and how experience took on the wildly poetic and runic echoes of those mystics who turned interiority into rooms, and landscapes, and worlds, fully inhabited with figures great and small. I came, I believe, from a generation of readers. The visual came to us through the word, took hold, took *flight*, in the imagination.

When reading literature goes the way of landlines, when careerism trumps the gathering of rosebuds, we get lurkers and dirty basements instead of cosmic delights that, for a moment, illumine the vast infinity of what is, finally, the ordinary. There, where the second sight of the body's wisdom is articulated beyond knowing, where the scrim of other worlds keeps faith with our deepest longings and intuitions, arousal becomes enlightenment.

In the virtual world, the status of the body is up for grabs. Lolita is a fulsome but two-dimensional image on a Facebook page. Not unhappily, then, I shall bid her adieu and cast my lot with Nabokov.

I have come full circle.

From the Faraway, Nearby

Georgia O'Keeffe to Alfred Stieglitz [Abiquiu, NM to Lake George, NY]

You have not seen it,
so you want me always
to paint flowers. You,

east in the lake house
while I am in the desert,
which is not a place of light

on things but things in
light—a country of form,
of beauty shorn.

There is no middle
ground. Fore
and back collapse

into a single plane.
When I am not here
I am on my way back.

To the scalded hills,
the flare-bleached bones.
To loneliness, calcified.

I paint a deer skull
with too many points,
as though bone could grow

to particular adventure:
I scale the hills, scalp twitching
with velvet of first antler.

what if my kind formed a grange & decided to seed the world?

between signifying
& saying nothing

raz & de-raz-
      innate

we of the post-raz &
      post-rez

share
Rocinante's fate

get stuck in Quixote's
quicksanded dreams

pathetic & pathétique

unwanted uhthers
your secret luhvers

we of the holy graft
the hybridized seed

grainA rubbed into grainB
now Roundup Ready

our new mixt-raza's
strong enough

      to take it

on both / all chins
      can threaten

to tip the scales
change the global %

of who is < or >

     no more
round up the usual…

one size fits all
kara walker cameos

of history
in black & white

primitive yin / yang
slavers & enslaved

     nosssiree
buddha-bubba

we are
the sepia-toned

     raza
of rung-ruiners

globetrotting
hawkers of

ka-ching &
    I Ching

& what can brown
    do for you

two dimensions
cannot hold us

we run in circles
you cannot see

in agar jelly from
the hanging tree

we are
mr & ms pac-tan

pack mules
       gone viral

mutating
micro-biologics

superlative
superbugs

& we plan to eat
all y'all

long live
La Pax Mulatta

Mystery of the Narcissistic Impulse

Rose wakens from a night of dreams in which she flew kites with the Queen of England. The Queen offered her a breakfast of kippers in exchange for the gift of a blue straw hat. Rose floats between continents of reality, the clock blinking 3:59, 4:00, 4:01 in a river of digitized time. Following the Queen's orders, she tries to sleep by counting sheep; at number 60 she glances at the clock again: 4:30. She slides out of bed, pulls on her chenille robe, grabs her glasses, and heads for the kitchen to make coffee.

Her partner Ann, already up, announces the weather report: "Clearing today, more rain due by the weekend."

Rose kisses her wrinkled cheek. "Have you noticed the narcissus blooming?"

"What's a narcissus?" Ann looks blank, her eyelids fluttering like new-hatched butterflies.

"A kind of daffodil, but smaller. They line the path to the front door."

"Those." Ann stiffens. "They get in my way when I come in from the car. Can I cut them down?"

Rose tightens the belt on her robe. "I'll take care of it." She retreats into her wingback chair, sips coffee, picks up a mystery novel, only to discover at the end of Chapter One no murder has yet taken place. All good mysteries featured murder in the first chapter. At the end of her life's Chapter One, at the age of 18, a murder occurred, and murderous deeds became a habit.

The first, a strangulation of her developing self by a rush into early marriage in the name of maturity—a crime of intemperate passion. The second, premeditated over two decades, a clean chop to sever herself from that marriage. Her husband, though wounded, survived. She killed her sexual interest in men, embraced lesbianism, and transferred her attention to women.

Her teenage self, lurking for years in her limbic system like a sullen P.O.W. and now freed from confinement, threw her into fresh new adventures. Canoeing down the Russian River. Swinging on a rope over a deep and thorny canyon. Flirting audaciously at lesbian dances. Reading lesbian porn. Answering the lesbian personal ads. Sampling various types of stimulating erotica.

Staring out the window, Rose sees nothing but pre-dawn darkness, as if looking inside her own brain. A July Fourth sparkler of remembrance: her entry into an alternative woman's world, a secret society hidden beneath the mundane one. There she consorted with sado-masochists, diesel dykes, femmes, stone butches, certified lesbians, political lesbians, transsexual lesbians, those transitioning through gender options, and those who resisted any label, which made it difficult for the many lesbian librarians.

Her first lover, a newly out butch, wanted a family much like the one Rose had fled; her second turned out to be untrustworthy. Now she's settled in with her third, a sincere, old-fashioned, ex-military sergeant who understands flowers only in the context of indoor bouquets. Straight or gay, relationships were problematic, though the power dynamic was a more even match in lesbian circles.

Even after all these adventures seeking love, guilt stalks her: the guilt of divorce, knowledge of her imperfections as a mother, not to mention the sin of failure to become the popular debutante her mother wished her to be. She does not regret ending the marriage, though guilt clings to her decision like cobwebs.

She wrestles herself from cobwebs back to the morning. Narcissus: Greek youth falls in love with the reflection he sees smiling back at him from a forest pool. A morality tale about the dangers of self-involvement, or perhaps it was about homosexual love. Freud turned the myth into a mental condition, an obsession with the image of the self. One could never be sure about Freud and his murky language, an overgrowth of algae destroying the clarity of Narcissus's pool.

Love stories based on myths burdened with neurotic theories disappoint Rose. Another disappointment arrived with the children: recognition of boundaries to her freedom. But then the boundaries turned out to be mythological also, vernal pools that dry up in summer and disappear. When the storytellers went home, Narcissus's forest pool could have dried up like one of those. After weeks of staring at his slowly receding face he fell asleep, the weather warmed, he keeled over into the muddy hole and suffered a concussion of consciousness rather than a drowning in self-regard.

Time ticks past Rose's chair, alerting her to refocus on the novel in her lap. It is full of description and dense with the minute details of everyday life. Murder did occur, she learns in Chapter Two, but sometime in the past. Revenge is planned for the near future by a large cohort of varied victims. London provides the setting, during a prolonged rainstorm. Rose stayed in London for one evening, on the way back from a tour of Cotswolds Gardens. Her tour group spent 15 days tramping through the rain to view one garden after another. She enjoyed the trip, but was it worth the cost? Walking about under dripping umbrellas. Flowers of early summer not yet in bloom, and spring bulbs past their season.

Ann says Rose is too concerned about money. She implies this is a Jewish trait; she herself is a Christian who converses with a Higher Power. What if, Rose wonders, Narcissus, staring into his watery eyes, experienced a religious epiphany? He met his Higher Power, who warred against the reflection's Higher Power, like countries in the Middle East. A fight between twins, they focused on each other's worst traits, unsatisfied with the good ones. She thought of the two voices in her brain constantly arguing.

Rose puts aside the book when Ann hands her the morning paper. Wars and military actions consume pages of newsprint. She prefers to focus on gardening rather than the numbers of dead and maimed piling up around the world. Blackberry vines push up everywhere, irises bloom in reds and purples. Gophers move in from their winter hideouts. Not much can be done about stopping the wars popping up around the globe, but the garden is controllable, after a fashion. She spends hours planting new seedlings of lettuce, cabbage, and Brussels sprouts, and smashing the many snails that ate them. Acknowledging the flowers blooming, she silently encourages them to persevere a few more days.

Rose's brother calls from Los Angeles, 800 miles away. Their 90-year-old mother, who lives near him, is in the hospital due to an allergic reaction to asthma medication that a doctor prescribed to clear up the cough she's had for the past ten years. A urinary tract infection was found, which led to an ultrasound test because doctors suspected something more serious.

At dinnertime her brother calls again. He spoke to the doctor in charge, who knew nothing of the cough, the allergic reaction, or the infection. He thinks it's a gall bladder problem, but two tests have not confirmed it. An MRI is scheduled for tomorrow. If he finds what he's looking for, it could mean an operation. Rose does not trust doctors who don't know what other doctors have said. "Is the doctor not finding a problem where he expected," she asks, "like Bush not finding the weapons he expected in Iraq?"

"Don't go there," her brother replies.

Flocks of goldfinches and house finches appear the next day, perching in the apple tree near the bird feeder. A small hawk flies to the top of a cottonwood, picking out a target for its lunch. Her brother calls: doctors retrieved two gallstones; no operation needed for now. Though happy with this news, Rose wonders about the future. Don't go there, her brother said. The future holds possibility of negative outcomes. A-void. When their mother was pulled out of the MRI tube, her brother says, she said to the nurses, "Thanks for the ride."

Rose stays awake after dinner by composing on the computer while her partner watches game shows. She writes the story of herself because she wants to know if her life is entertaining or strange or routine. Is there a trajectory with a beginning, a middle, and an end of interest to anyone? What is the point, the crisis, the denouement, the satisfying resolution, or is the point merely to live it? Writing itself requires constant editing; like a spider, the writer spins out a web of words and then resides in them, continually fussing with and mending the broken threads.

She suspects writing about one's life is a narcissistic impulse, and the real motivation for murder number two, when she killed her marriage. She opted for self-preservation. So few sanctioned roles for women, who were labeled well or badly depending on how they supported their men, or didn't. Tiresome to be caged that way.

Narcissus, a novice when it came to love, was at the mercy of the mirror, constantly checking his face for blemishes. Then Echo appeared. She fell in love with him, but he paid her no attention; she faded away, except for her voice. Once she became vocal, no one could make her stop. Rose was harangued through her youth by her mother for not speaking up, and later by her husband for not holding conversations with him, the kind that kept his mind relaxed and at peace. When she decided to talk, he said she brought up the wrong subjects. She couldn't help that the words poured out chaotically, so unused was she to speaking. Her narcissistic impulse morphed into an echo-istic one, which exhausted itself in the discourse of 1970s consciousness-raising feminism. All this reflection on reflection makes Rose's head hurt, like being out by the ocean on a sunny day without sunglasses—blinded by reflection, or maybe it's simply that she reads too much; her mother criticized her for that.

Rose has a part-time job at the tourist office of her coastal town, where she provides information to travelers. Afterward, she drives her pickup truck down the road to the bluffs to watch the waves crashing against rocks as she eats her lunch. The FedEx man is there too, and a woman who reads a book instead of watching the waves. Rose stares at the ocean; it reminds her of her mother's smothering intent. She rolls down the window to breathe the salt-laden air. Young gulls watch. Will she throw out a bit of sandwich for them? "There is no free lunch in this world," her father would say when his children wanted something.

During the night Rose dreams of an old woman dressed in a long wool coat. Mrs. Dungeness Crab, who sleeps on a cot in a Red Cross shelter while the city is bombed. Mrs. Crab awakens in the dark, frightened; she wants to go home. Her eyes meet Rose's and she stares into them with a kind look on her face. At dawn, when Rose's eyelids struggle to open, she knows she is fully awake. Her left eyelid often refuses to open, and she massages it in an encouraging way. Mrs. Crab follows her when she rises from bed.

Rose goes to a nursery sale and buys fifteen plants, then walks through her garden figuring out where to put them. After hours of weeding, digging, planting, and pushing the wheelbarrow, her back is painfully sore. It is difficult to bend, to unbend. Mrs. Dungeness Crab haunts her throughout the day with that kind smile, or is it, rather, wry? She reminds Rose of an angel she saw in a movie, who came to escort the movie hero to heaven. The time will come for Rose to be escorted, too. She'd better get everything planted, because in a few years she won't be able to do any real gardening. Her knees will stiffen, her back weaken further, and she will wander through her garden like a wraith wrapped in a shawl staring at the fertile weeds and unable to do a damned thing about it. She can hear Ann say, "I told you so," and demanding she stay inside to prevent a chill.

Rain comes and lingers for days. Rose, back in her chair, finishes her first mystery and begins another. A dead body is discovered in the first chapter, and the murderer confesses in the last. As with the other mystery, the story takes place in England, but not in London. It includes an AIDS victim, an idiot, a young widow, and a handsome police detective taking lessons to convert to Judaism. The idiot, the most interesting character, reveals momentary bursts of innate wisdom. Rose suffers from the opposite problem. Her brain's intelligence is quite sufficient, but idiocy leaks out at inopportune moments. Her mother called her dumb, and even her partner hints at Rose's stupidity.

The New Yorker arrives every Friday, an airlift of food for the starving. It is rife, these days, with stories from or about Iraq. Reporters describe the U.S. as the new Roman Empire, and she knows how that ended. She knows who owns the "weapons of mass destruction"—why can't they just call it what it is: the A-bomb, the H-bomb, the X, Y, Z of annihilation of civilization as we know it. It won't be the end of the world; the planet will survive. After all, it was born out of atomic reactions; the universe is one big exploding mass of shrapnel flying through the aftermath of destruction.

One evening her brother calls to report their last aunt has died. She was younger than their mother; she still had her wits about her.

"You always call with bad news," Rose says.

"It's my job," he says. "She phoned a few months ago and was fine then. She told me she was lonely."

"And now she has died of it."

"Can't you accept that people die of old age?"

"No," says Rose, and hangs up. Their mother solves the loneliness problem by retreating from the closed-in world of the frail, aged widow to enter the world of decades past, peopled by the dead. Dad is just upstairs, she says; if she could climb the stairs he'd be there. Her mother lives a zombie life, giving up the fading world of now for the non-world of what she imagines. Perhaps a blessing that she's half blind and very deaf.

Ann nags Rose about the cluttered state of their kitchen counters. Why did she marry a woman like her mother, Rose wonders. She spent her life trying to escape Mom. *It is an opportunity*, comes the answer from out of the air, *to re-shape your past*. Ah, opportunity. She could flee (she visualizes the futile, panicked flight of the Pompeians during the eruption of Mt. Vesuvius, significantly like what Ann's angry outbursts would be if Rose ever voiced a suggestion of leaving). Better to stay. It's the easier choice.

Rain lasts for a week. Tall irises bloom one after another on their thick stalks with no one to appreciate them except the voracious snails. The pond overflows. Birds bathe in water-filled buckets. Weeds advance into the flowerbeds. Rose reads a history about the slaughter of Roman legions by Germanic tribes in 9 A.D., how they led the Roman soldiers into a forest and then ambushed them. That was years before the Visigoths overran Rome. Rose considers how walls are built as defenses, and how easily breached they are. The way stone crumbles, like untended memories hanging on a disintegrating peg of a neuron. The fragility of civilization, so easily torn—a human construct, subject to relationships.

That evening, reading a book in bed as Ann slumbers beneath three layers of nightclothes and two quilts, she stops to ponder war. Is war, that is, murder on a grand scale, a genetic defect built into the human genome, something akin to lemming panic? Is war a self-propagating instinct left over from the age of the dinosaurs? If all earthlings were female would it make any difference? She holds her partner's warm hand with her cold one and waits for sleep, reminded of the kind anesthesiologist who prepares the patient for surgery.

Mrs. Crab walks on a stony beach. The sea becomes red at dawn. White cliffs of Dover gleam in the distance. Shattered bullets turn to sand. The Queen slides down among the rocks looking for a foothold. Mrs. Crab shows the way, to a garden all green and brown and cold where anemones flutter their purple arms. The Queen doffs her blue straw hat. "Sleep!" she orders. Five sheep fall down. The butler sweeps them away with a flourish.

For you, who would have us

in bed late with the New York times and lazy morning sun. Five
minutes out the door and the car always sparkling. Spicy Ma Po tofu
in beautiful bowls, artisanal beer in glasses precisely warmed. A trip
to Mozambique just because. I give you tiny girls who will make you
cry over their fickle hearts. I give you three changes of clothes and a
screaming fit before breakfast. Endless nights of pasta with cheese and
nothing else. Tap water to wash it down. I give you piss and shit and
vomit: on the bed, on your clothes, in your hair. The peddling of feet
in the small of your back at midnight. I give you daughters.